How to Take Control of Your "Yes" and "Nos"

A Step-by-Step Guide on How to Take Charge of Your Life

By

Pst. Blake Dwight

Copyright ©2023 Pst. Blake Dwight
All Rights Reserved

All rights reserved. No part of this publication may be reproduced, distributed, or transmitted in any form or by any means, including photocopying, recording, or other electronic or mechanical methods, without the prior written permission of the publisher, except in the case of brief quotations embodied in critical reviews and certain other noncommercial uses permitted by copyright law.

Names, characters, places, and incidents used in this book are resemblance to actual events or locales or persons, living or dead, which are entirely coincidental.

Table of Contents

Introduction 6
Chapter 1 10
   The Power of Choice 10
      Understanding the Impact of Your Decisions 12
      The Art of Saying "Yes" with Purpose 15
      When to Say "No" for Your Well-being 18
Chapter 2 24
   Building Your Decision-Making Framework 24
      Setting Clear Goals and Priorities 26
      Developing a Personal Values System 30
      Balancing Short-term Gratification and Long-term Goals 33
Chapter 3 38
   Mastering the Art of Saying "Yes" 38
      Effective Communication and Assertiveness 40
      Negotiation Strategies for Win-Win Outcomes 43
      Overcoming the Fear of Missing Out (FOMO) 47
Chapter 4 52
   The Art of Saying "No" Gracefully 52
      Setting Boundaries in Your Personal and Professional Life .. 53
      Strategies for Declining Requests and Invitations ... 56
      Handling Rejection and Disappointment 60
Chapter 5 64
   Taking Charge of Your Life 64
      Creating a Decision Journal for Self-awareness 65
      The Role of Resilience in Decision-making 69

Navigating Life Transitions with Confidence 73

Conclusion 78

Introduction

Uncertainty hung over me like a heavy fog, blocking the way forward as I stood at the fork in the road of my life. Every decision seemed important at the time, and every "yes" or "no" appeared to reverberate across my future. It was a vital moment. This is the account of how I came to understand the power of my "yes" and "no" and how I set out on a transformative quest to seize control of my future.

I wanted for clarity in a world filled with demands and options, where every choice can result in a different outcome. I yearned to comprehend the significant impact of my decisions—positive and negative—both. To welcome possibilities that were actually in line with my goals, I yearned for the capacity to say "yes" with intention. At the same time, I required the ability to know when to say "no" in order to protect my time, energy, and wellbeing.

The journey I took to explore the art and science of decision-making is documented in this book. This trip passes through the regions of individual values, goal-setting, assertive communication, and resilience. Through struggles and successes, I learned the techniques and methods that enable us to take charge of our lives, one decision at a time.

As we set out on this journey together, come along with me as I share the insights I've gained and the lessons I've learnt. So that we can all confidently move into the life we picture, let's uncover the techniques for mastering the dance between "yes" and "no." This is a tale of personal growth, empowerment, and the profound understanding that our decisions have a huge impact on our futures.

Chapter 1

The Power of Choice

Each thread of our life's tapestry is woven with a decision—a choice that places us on a specific course and establishes the tones and outlines of our existence. Hello and welcome to "The Power of Choice," the first part of our adventure.

Life is a complex mosaic of choices, from the unimportant to the profound. We are presented with a variety of alternatives from the moment we wake up until we put our heads down, and each one has the potential to have negative effects. Have you ever stopped to consider the significant impact these decisions have on our life, though?

In this chapter, we go into the very core of choice, comprehending its importance and recognizing the enormous influence it has on our journey. We'll examine the skill of saying "yes" with intention, accepting opportunities that support our goals, and finding the strength to use the liberating word "no" when it's required for our wellbeing.

Get ready to explore the complexities of decision-making, to understand what motivates us to make a choice, and to consider how each decision affects the chapters that follow. Keep in mind that the pen is in our hands as we begin this investigation of "The Power of

Choice" and that our choices are what give our lives their meaning.

Understanding the Impact of Your Decisions

Every decision we make sends a stone into the pond of our life, and that stone causes ripples that go far beyond the moment of choosing. It is simple to underestimate the breadth and depth of these ripples, but realizing the enormous significance of our choices is the key to regaining control over our "yes" and "no."

The Domino Effect

Think of a row of dominoes representing choices, each one standing tall. We tap the initial domino when we decide something, which starts a domino effect. Our circumstances, connections, and possibilities are impacted by the long-term effects of that first decision.

Take accepting a new job offer into consideration. It can result in a change in daily routine, new coworkers who become friends, or even a move to a different place. The change in employment is not the only thing that might happen. Our families, our free time, and even our sense of identity are all impacted by these consequences as they spread into our personal life.

The Butterfly Effect

According to the fabled butterfly effect, a butterfly's wing flap in Brazil might cause a tornado to erupt in Texas. Similar to how a seemingly inconsequential decision can lead to big consequences.

For instance, making the simple decision to start an exercise regimen can result in better health, more vitality, and the self-assurance to seize new chances.

The Weight of Regret

When we look back with the benefit of hindsight, we sometimes only fully understand the effects of our choices. One of life's most effective teachers is regret. We can get very concerned about the paths not traveled, the chances passed up, or the erroneous turns taken. This emphasizes how critical it is to make deliberate, informed decisions.

Let us keep in mind that each "yes" and "no" we say or don't say adds to the mosaic of our lives as we travel its terrain. We shall examine how to deliberate about these decisions, coordinating them with our beliefs, objectives, and aspirations, in the upcoming chapters. By being aware of the effects of our actions, we build a future that will be shaped by our purposeful decisions.

The Art of Saying "Yes" with Purpose

The power of the word "yes" is enormous. It's a gateway to fresh encounters, chances, and connections. However, unintentionally saying "yes" might result in overextending yourself, exhaustion, and a loss of concentration on what's really important. The ability to say "yes" with intention is a talent that can change the course of our life.

Aligning With Your Goals

We devote our time, effort, and resources when we say "yes" to anything. It's essential to match these commitments with our objectives in order for them to have meaning. Consider how the offer aligns with your goals before saying "yes" to it. Does it advance you toward your goals? Does it fit with your values? Your "yes" becomes a step forward as opposed to a diversion when it is in line with your objectives.

Setting Boundaries

Saying "yes" doesn't mean accepting everything. Setting up boundaries gives you the power to make decisions that respect your priorities and well-being. Set boundaries to prevent your time and resources from getting used up on commitments that don't support your goals. You can only practice self-respect and self-care if you say "yes" to your own boundaries.

Embracing the Right Opportunities

Many of the opportunities in the world are not intended for us. In order to make wise decisions, practice discernment. If an opportunity has the potential to change your life, think about how it might do so and decide if it aligns with your passion and purpose. When the appropriate opportunity presents itself, saying "yes" might occasionally lead to unexpected opportunities.

Saying "No" to say "Yes"

In an ironic twist, refusing something might be one of the most effective methods to affirm what is most important. You free up valuable time and resources to invest in activities that lead to fulfillment and growth by declining commitments that don't support your objectives. You gain the power to control the story of your life when you learn how to say "no" politely.

We set out on an intentional journey as we develop the skill of saying "yes" with intention. Every "yes" adds to the masterpiece we are creating by acting as a brushstroke on the canvas of our lives.

When to Say "No" for Your Well-being

The letter "no" plays a significant part in the symphony of life, acting as a rest note that promotes harmony. Knowing when to say "no" is just as important as knowing how to say "yes" with intention. For the benefit of your wellbeing, this chapter is devoted to helping you recognize when to use that potent, two-letter word.

Preserving Your Energy

The way we distribute our limited energy has major consequences. Each "yes" we say and each commitment we make uses some of our limited energy. When we say "no" to some requests, we save our energy for things and people who really feed our spirit. It's a deliberate effort to keep your energy up and avoid burnout.

Setting Boundaries

Establishing boundaries in your life starts with saying "no." Limits that safeguard your mental, emotional, and physical health are called boundaries rather than barriers. You are reaffirming your self-worth and commitment to your own well-being when you say "no" to things that cross these boundaries. Your needs are affirmed to be as significant to everyone else's.

Honoring Your Priorities

Multiple demands competing for our attention make life a perpetual juggling act. We need to choose our obligations carefully if we want to live truly and in accordance with our objectives and ideals. An act of self-respect is to say "no" to requests that don't align with your priorities. It involves choosing your path over someone else's expectations.

Embracing "No" as a Complete Sentence

You don't always need to give detailed justifications for your choices. The answer "No" is a complete sentence. You can avoid overcommitting and the sense that you have to defend your decisions if you learn to use it with confidence. It's a strategy for expressing your control over your decisions.

Managing Guilt and Expectations

Society frequently puts tremendous pressure on us to be flexible and to please others. When we say "no," this could make us feel guilty. It's important to understand that your wellbeing counts, and that, when required, saying "no" is an act of self-care rather than selfishness. The art of saying "no" requires a thorough understanding of and control over these emotions.

Remember that it's not about being nasty or closed off as we discuss when to say "no" for your wellbeing. It's about living a balanced, satisfying life where your "no" opens the door for more significant "yeses." It's a journey toward regaining your time, energy, and happiness, one wise "no" at a time.

Chapter 2

Building Your Decision-Making Framework

We are at a critical point in our quest to gain control over our "yes" and "no," and we are about to enter a new chapter. If Chapter 1 showed us how to say "yes" with intention and when to firmly say "no" for our wellbeing, Chapter 2 gives us the skills we need to create a solid framework for making choices that are in line with our goals.

The decisions we make throughout our life make up a mosaic, but not every option is the same. Others misdirect us, while some help us move closer to our goals. We require a decision-making compass, a tool that guides us in plotting the course to our preferred destination, to assist us navigate this complex web of possibilities.

We'll investigate this compass's parts in this chapter. In this section, we'll discuss how to define priorities and goals that are clear, develop a system of values that are unique to you, and strike a delicate balance between what you want now and what you want in the long run. At the conclusion of this voyage, you will have a solid framework for making decisions that will help you navigate the maze of options and make sure that each "yes" and "no" is a step in the direction of the future you want.

So get ready to set out on a voyage of introspection and strategic choice. The framework we create for making decisions gives us a strong tool that enables us to take control of our future with assurance and clarity.

Setting Clear Goals and Priorities

The foundation of distinct goals and priorities is at the core of good decision-making. The same way a ship needs a goal and a map to cruise the broad ocean, we also need to have a direction in mind as we move across the huge field of options.

1. The Power of Clarity: Take a moment to picture yourself in the middle of a deep forest with no obvious way out. Every move seems arbitrary, and

it's disconcerting. Imagine the same situation, but now add a map and a clearly marked trail. You've got direction and a goal all of a sudden. This illustrates how clearly defining your life's objectives and goals can transform it.

2. Defining Your North Star: A Definition Your North Star, which directs your course through life, is comprised of your goals. Focus, meaning, and inspiration are provided by them. You must first decide what actually important to you in order to harness the power of your "yes" and "no." What long-term objectives do you have? What kind of legacy would you be happy to leave behind? Your decisions have significance when they are guided by your goals, which also aid in deciding which opportunities to seize and which to pass up.

3. Setting Objective Priorities: Like options, not all objectives are created equal. Choosing which objectives are most important in your life at any given time is the art of prioritization. The importance and urgency of each objective must be determined. You can organize your time and resources more wisely and make decisions that are more focused and effective by knowing what your priorities are.

4. Avoiding Decision Fatigue: The modern world constantly presents us with options, from what to wear to what career path to choose. When we are presented with an excessive number of options, decision fatigue can set in, which can result in bad decisions. Clear goals and priorities serve as a

filter, simplifying options and easing the mental strain of decision-making.

5. Making a Roadmap: The lines connecting your priorities and goals constitute your life's road map. You join these dots with each decision you make, constructing a path that embodies your particular journey. You are less likely to wander off course when you have a plan in place. You take control of your future and create a life that aligns with your ideals and aspirations.

You will have a road map by the end of this chapter that not only directs your choices but also reveals the way to a more meaningful and fulfilling life.

Developing a Personal Values System

As we continue on our path through the art of decision-making, we reach a crucial turning point: creating a system of personal values. Our values act as a compass, showing us the way through life, much like our objectives and priorities do.

1. The Essence of Values: Values are the fundamental tenets that characterize who we are and what we stand for. They are the unseen threads that are sewn into the fabric of who we are. Making decisions that align with our real selves requires an understanding of and adherence to our beliefs.

2. Aligning With Your Values: As a filter through which every decision must pass, consider your

values. You feel a strong sense of authenticity and contentment when your actions are in line with your ideals. However, when you behave in a way that goes against your moral principles, dissonance develops, which is uncomfortable and causes internal conflict.

3. The Role of Self-Discovery: It takes effort and continual self-discovery to create a personal values system. It entails thinking critically about your beliefs, determining the values that are most important to you, and evaluating how those values affect the decisions you make. Knowing your values and your uncompromising principles is important.

4. Values as Decision-Making Anchors: Values serve as a compass in the turbulent sea of life's decisions.

They keep you anchored and enable you to weather storms with purpose and resiliency. Take your values into account when making decisions. It respects your values, right? Does it accurately reflect who you want to be?

5. Integrity and Consistency: Integrity comes from living in accordance with your values. When your behavior mirrors your convictions, it suggests you are acting morally. Your self-esteem is raised by being consistent, and you gain the respect and trust of others as a result.

We went into great detail about how to create a system of personal values. By the end of this chapter, you will have a better grasp of who you are and how your values can act as a beacon, directing you toward actions that are both purposeful and deeply meaningful.

Balancing Short-term Gratification and Long-term Goals

We frequently come to a crossroads in the broad fabric of life where the pursuit of long-term goals and the attraction of instant fulfillment collide. This tight line between balance and self-awareness is a key concept in the art of decision-making.

1. The Tug of Instant Gratification: The desire for instant gratification and pleasure is ingrained in human nature. It is the feeling of satisfaction we get from giving in to our wishes, from the alluring nibble to the impulsive purchase. Although they

give us immediate pleasure, these moments might occasionally make us lose sight of our long-term goals.

2. The Benefits of Delayed Gratification: Delayed gratification, which is the capacity to withstand the pull of immediate benefits in favor of bigger, more important goals, is on the other end of the scale. It's the self-control to put off immediate pleasure in favor of something more worthwhile later, like setting money aside for a fantasy vacation or making investments in one's own growth.

3. Harmonizing Short-term and Long-term: Finding a perfect balance between immediate gratification and long-term objectives is the secret to making decisions that are both wise and productive. Making decisions that respect your immediate

needs without sacrificing your long-term goals is an art.

4. Developing a Decision Matrix: One effective method for striking this balance is to create a decision matrix. Examining both the immediate and long-term effects of a decision is part of it. You can decide what to do in a way that is in line with your overall goals by comparing the potential long-term benefits against the short-term gains.

5. Strengthening Self-control: Self-control and discipline are frequently needed when juggling short-term and long-term concerns. Making decisions that are in your best interests over the long term requires strengthening these qualities. Maintaining motivation can be aided by techniques

like creating rewards for reaching milestones on your long-term goals.

We've looked at practical ways to control impulsive behavior, methods for establishing and accomplishing long-term goals, and the psychology of delayed gratification. Keep using these strategies to balance short-term satisfaction with long-term objectives.

Chapter 3

Mastering the Art of Saying "Yes"

The answer "yes" frequently carries the promise of exploration, opportunity, and personal development in life's complex dance. How frequently yet do we stop to consider the magnitude of this one little word's influence on our path? Thank you for reading this chapter, which examines the art of expressing "yes" in all its complexity and richness.

Saying "yes" is more than just an affirmation; it is a skill, a way of thinking, and a means of enhancing one's life and career. In order to realize the full potential of this affirmative term, we will set out on a trip in this chapter.

The areas of successful communication, negotiation, and the psychology of affirmations will all be covered in depth.

The ability to say "yes" with confidence involves more than just using the word; it also involves embracing possibilities that are consistent with your aims and values while overcoming anxiety and self-doubt. It's about balancing your affirmative responses with your wider life narrative.

So, as we enter the "yes" realm, get ready to discover all of its nuances. Together, we will work through the complexities, learning how to say "yes" with thought and purpose, converting it from a casual response into a potent tool for sculpting the life you want.

Effective Communication and Assertiveness

Effective communication and assertiveness are essential for getting a "yes" from someone. Beyond the simple act of saying something, the way we express our affirmation and self-aggrandize has a significant influence on the results and connections that materialize.

1. Clarity and Consistency: Clarity at the heart of effective communication. Be absolutely certain of your objective before responding "yes." Conflicting expectations and misunderstandings can result from ambiguity. Don't forget to communicate consistently as well. Your affirmative responses have to be consistent

throughout time in reflecting your values and priorities.

2. The Power of Confidence: Communicating effectively requires assertiveness. Getting your "yes" through with assurance and conviction is important. A firm "yes" conveys assurance, which builds credibility and respect. Be mindful that being confident does not mean being haughty; rather, it means expressing your willingness with composure.

3. Setting Boundaries Within Affirmatives: Even when responding with affirmatives, assertiveness still entails creating boundaries. Just as with saying "no," saying "yes" shouldn't entail sacrificing your wellbeing or your morals. The ability to accept opportunities that support your goals while staying

true to yourself depends on your ability to be assertive in your affirmative responses.

4. Managing Expectations: Whether it be professionally or emotionally, when you say "yes," you are making obligations. Regarding what you can and cannot deliver, it is crucial to be practical. Stress and burnout can be brought on by overcommitting out of a fear of disappointing others. To create a healthy balance, be clear in your communication about your talents and control expectations.

5. Negotiating and Collaboration: In negotiations and teamwork, clear communication and firmness are essential. Make sure there are open lines of communication when you say "yes" to a project, assignment, or opportunity. Ensure that the phrases

fit your skills and objectives by being open to discussion and collaboration.

Your compass will be effective communication and assertiveness as you set out to perfect the skill of saying "yes." By developing these abilities, you not only improve the quality of your relationships, but you also open the door for positive reactions that promote both individual and mutual growth. It's important to remember that how you say "yes" is just as important as whether or not you decide to say it.

Negotiation Strategies for Win-Win Outcomes

Negotiation frequently serves as a link between your affirmative response and a result that benefits both parties in the complex art of expressing "yes." A simple "yes" can become a potent tool for developing win-win circumstances through skillful negotiation.

1. Understanding the Win-Win Philosophy: At its core, negotiation ought to aim for a win-win result. This way of thinking is based on the idea that both sides may come to an agreement and end the negotiation happy. When you approach discussions with a win-win perspective, it lays the groundwork for cooperation rather than conflict.
2. Effective Listening: Active listening is one of the most effective negotiation techniques. It is essential to genuinely comprehend the requirements, wishes, and worries of the other side. Your ability to modify your "yes" to fit their

interests when you actively listen will increase the likelihood of a successful outcome.

3. Clarifying Expectations: Different expectations frequently cause misunderstandings. If you answer "yes," be sure to make all terms of the agreement clear. Discussing deadlines, roles, and potential hiccups is part of this. The bargaining process will go more smoothly if you are clearer up front.

4. Offering and Requesting Concessions: There is a give and take in negotiations. Prepare yourself to make compromises that advance both your objectives and those of the other party. Likewise, don't be afraid to ask for modifications that will make your "yes" more valuable. Concessions are the dance's steps since negotiation is a dance.

5. Alternative Solutions: Sometimes it may not be possible to respond with a simple "yes" because of numerous limitations. In these situations, look into alternate options that still benefit both sides. Unexpected win-win outcomes can be produced by being flexible and creative.

6. Building Long-Term Relationships: Building long-lasting relationships is an important part of effective negotiation, in addition to the current agreement. The bargaining process should be cooperative and respectful. It creates the foundation for any future cooperation when both sides depart feeling satisfied.

Remember that saying "yes" isn't just about accepting or agreeing; it's also about creating affirmative replies that open the door to growth, collaboration, and mutual benefit as we navigate the landscape of negotiation methods for win-win outcomes. You may use your "yes" as a powerful instrument to shape favorable outcomes in both your personal and professional life by becoming an expert negotiator.

Overcoming the Fear of Missing Out (FOMO)

The fear of missing out (FOMO) has grown to be a significant factor in the modern world and affects our choices. This anxiety can create impulsive "yeses," in which we accept opportunities not because they support our objectives but rather out of a fear of missing out on something worthwhile or exciting.

Understanding FOMO

The fear of missing out on opportunities, connections, or experiences—or FOMO—is a widespread emotion that results from our continual exposure to the well managed lives of others on social media. We frequently respond "yes" impulsively because of this.

The Impact on Decision-Making

FOMO can have a significant effect on our decision-making. It might cause us to take on too much, dividing our attention across too many activities and lowering the standard of our commitments. Additionally, it may impair our capacity to choose actions that are actually consistent with our objectives and ideals.

Strategies to Overcome FOMO

To perfect the skill of saying "yes" with intention, one must learn to overcome FOMO. To assist you overcome this fear, try these methods:

1. Mindfulness: Develop mindfulness so that you can remain in the moment and recognize the importance of the decisions you make. Realize that oftentimes, saying "yes" to one thing also implies saying "no" to another.
2. Prioritization: Clarify your objectives and priorities before setting them. It is simpler to resist the pull of pursuits or opportunities that don't fit with your vision when you are clear about what is actually important to you.

3. JOMO (Joy of Missing Out): Move from FOMO to JOMO as your frame of reference. Don't be afraid to enjoy missing out on things that won't advance your goals or well-being.

4. Set Boundaries: Set up limits that will keep your focus, energy, and time safe. An effective strategy for combating FOMO is to learn to say "no" to obligations that are not absolutely necessary.

5. Reflect on Previous Encounters: Think back on occasions when you answered "yes" out of FOMO and evaluate the results. You'll frequently discover the concern was unwarranted and that you didn't miss anything important.

Embracing Purposeful Choices

Making decisions with a goal in mind will help you beat FOMO in the end. Thus, rather than being a response to fear, your "yes" becomes a deliberate step forward. You gain the ability to create a life that is full of worthwhile relationships and experiences.

Understanding and overcoming FOMO is an important step in the journey as we negotiate the subtleties of answering "yes." You are liberated from the constraints of rash choices, enabling you to positively react to possibilities that actually improve your life.

Chapter 4

The Art of Saying "No" Gracefully

Saying "no" politely is a skill that is frequently overlooked in the big drama of life's choices. This chapter digs deeply into the great art of declining with grace and compassion, of establishing boundaries that respect your wellbeing while fostering connections. "No" is more than simply a rejection; it's also a statement of one's value as a person, a pledge to take care of oneself, and a step toward honesty. Here, we look at how to say "no" in a way that turns it from a basic rejection into a potent instrument for upholding your beliefs, fostering relationships, and creating a life that is in line with your goals.

Setting Boundaries in Your Personal and Professional Life

Our personal and professional environments are limited by boundaries, which are like invisible walls. This chapter focuses on the skill of setting boundaries elegantly, which is essential to saying "no" to people with empathy and respect while maintaining your wellbeing.

1. The Importance of Boundaries: Healthy relationships and a balanced lifestyle are built on boundaries. In doing so, they ensure that your wants and values are respected by defining what is and is not acceptable. Defined boundaries are essential to mutual respect and productive

communication in both the personal and professional realms.

2. Defining Your Boundaries: With self-awareness comes the ability to set boundaries. Think about your values, priorities, and comfort zones. What are your firm stand-points? What are your restrictions? You may determine your boundaries by being aware of these factors.

3. Communicating boundaries: It takes skill to clearly express your boundaries. It demands self-confidence, sympathy, and effective communication. Whenever you say "no," be truthful and considerate about your limitations. Kindly but firmly express your demands and goals.

4. Boundaries in Personal Life: Your identity and emotional wellbeing are protected by boundaries in

intimate interactions. Boundaries help you offer without losing yourself, whether it's with loved ones, close friends, or romantic partners.

5. Boundaries in Professional Life: Setting limits in the workplace is crucial for managing expectations and preserving a healthy work-life balance. By protecting your personal time, they help you concentrate on your work without being constantly interrupted and prevent burnout.

6. Adapting Boundaries: As conditions change, boundaries might change and become less rigid. To keep up with your changing demands and objectives, it is crucial to periodically evaluate and adjust your boundaries.

It is possible to create relationships and environments that respect your values and well-being by becoming an expert at setting boundaries in both your personal and professional life. This will help you say "no" more politely and will help you feel more in control. In order to live a more meaningful and balanced life, this section will show you how to assertively define and communicate your boundaries.

Strategies for Declining Requests and Invitations

When done with grace, declining requests and invitations is an art that enables you to say "no" politely while preserving respect and understanding. We explore useful methods for navigating these tricky situations in this section.

1. The Polite Decline: Often, the best course of action is to politely and simply decline. Thank them for the invitation or request and politely but firmly say no. For instance, "Thank you for thinking of me, but I won't be able to participate at this time."

2. The "No" Sandwich: Your denial will be placed between two affirmative statements using this strategy. Start with a good acknowledgement, then say "I decline," then end on a positive note. In this case, you might say, "I appreciate your offer, but I must reject at this time. You'll find another person who can help, I have no doubt about that.

3. Offer an Alternative: Offer your assistance in a new way, or recommend an alternative remedy, as appropriate. Even if you are unable to meet the

original request, doing so demonstrates your sincere desire to assist.

4. Express Your Prior Commitments: Existing commitments can sometimes be the cause of rejection. Emphasize that it's a matter of availability rather than preference by expressing this in a clear manner. I'd love to, but I have commitments from the past that conflict with this schedule, for example.

5. Stay Firm but Kind: It's important to refuse politely while yet being courteous and understanding. You don't want to muddy up your response by over-explaining or over-apologizing.

6. Buy Time: It's acceptable to ask for more time to think over a request if you're not sure about it or require some thought before responding. Due to

the lack of pressure, you are able to make a thoughtful choice.

7. Maintain Authenticity and Honesty: Honesty is the best approach when it is suitable. It is okay to say this honestly but graciously if the request disagrees with your priorities or core principles. Trust and understanding are fostered by authenticity.

8. Practice Self-Care: Keep in mind that exercising self-care by saying "no" is important. You may spend the time and energy to what is genuinely important to you by maintaining your limits.

You can politely deny requests and invites by using these techniques, all the while maintaining relationships and honoring your personal boundaries. For self-empowerment and keeping a balanced existence, learning the art of saying "no" is a strong weapon.

Handling Rejection and Disappointment

It's inevitable that you will run against "no" from other people in the complex dance of gently saying "no." Learning the art of saying "no" requires you to handle rejection and disappointment with composure and resiliency.

1. Understanding the Two Sides of "No": There are both givers and takers in the "no" world; it is not one-sided. You'll have to learn how to accept another person's refusal in addition to navigating the difficulties of declining politely.

2. Dealing with Disappointment: When a request or invitation is turned down, it's normal to feel disappointed or even irritated. Acknowledging these feelings and allowing yourself to experience them without holding yourself accountable are crucial.

3. Avoid Personalization: A request's or a person's worth isn't always reflected in a rejection. It frequently happens as a result of the priorities, obligations, or circumstances of the other person. The rejection shouldn't be personalized.

4. Seek Feedback: Seeking feedback for personal or professional progress is suitable in certain circumstances. Respecting the other person's time and limits while politely requesting constructive

input regarding the reasons your request was denied.

5. Maintain Perspective: Keep in mind that a single "no" doesn't determine your value or your chances of receiving other opportunities in the future. Focus on the numerous "yeses" that may be in store and keep a wider perspective.

6. Embrace Resilience: The capacity to overcome disappointment is resilience. Over time, one can develop this ability. Use rejection as a springboard for growth, practice self-compassion, and look for advice from friends or mentors.

7. Respect Boundaries: Recognize and respect other people's boundaries as you would your own. Accept the "no" you receive when someone

declines your request politely without forcing them.

8. Preserve Relationships: Relationships can be preserved by saying "no" just once. You can keep the connection intact if you continue to show respect and empathy for the other person's decisions.

9. Adapt and Pivot: A chance to adjust and change course after being rejected. A "no" might occasionally guide you toward chances that hold greater potential.

When you respond to rejection and disappointment with grace and resiliency, you not only protect your wellbeing but also promote positive interactions and keep the confidence to say "no" when it's essential. It's a fundamental part of the skill of deftly navigating the world of "no" and "yes."

Chapter 5

Taking Charge of Your Life

Seizing control of your future is an incredibly important skill that beckons to be mastered in the fabric of existence. To embrace the art of taking control of your life, this chapter urges you to set out on a journey of self-empowerment. This journey takes you to the center of self-determination, where you take control of your destiny and become the creator of your story. In this article, we examine the tactics, attitudes, and behaviors that give you the capacity to create a life that is consistent with your core aspirations and principles.

Creating a Decision Journal for Self-awareness

Self-awareness serves as your guide while you work to take control of your life. Understanding the why and how behind your decisions is essential since they serve as the cornerstones of your path. In order to develop this self-awareness, a decision journal is a potent tool.

What is a Decision Journal?

Keeping track of your decision-making process is done with a decision journal. It serves as a repository for the judgments you must make, the alternatives you weigh, and the influencing elements.

Why Keep a Decision Journal?

- Clarity: By requiring you to express your ideas and motives, it helps you make decisions with greater clarity.

- Learning: It is an excellent resource for learning. You can spot trends, biases, and areas for development by looking back on previous choices.

- Accountability: It makes you answerable for the decisions you make. It's simpler to accept responsibility for the results when you can understand the thought process underlying your choices.

Creating Your Decision Journal:

- Select a Format: Whether it's a paper journal, an electronic file, or a specific software, pick a format that works for you.
- Capture Key Details: Keep track of the circumstances, options you evaluated, your reasoning, and the elements that affected each decision you made.
- Reflect: Go back to your journal entries after some time has gone. Evaluate the results of your choices in light of your objectives and core principles.

Benefits of a Decision Journal:

- Enhanced Self-awareness: Your ideals, goals, and methods for making decisions become more clear to you.
- Better Decision-Making: When you have a better grasp of your own cognitive process, you can make more intelligent decisions.
- Growth and Adaptation: By reflecting on your past choices, you can become more adaptable and capable of making decisions that promote personal development.

It is a journey of self-discovery to keep a decision journal; it is not merely a recording exercise. Through this practice, you can cultivate self-awareness, which will enable you to live more purposefully and intentionally.

The Role of Resilience in Decision-making

A key component of making wise decisions is resilience, or the capacity to recover from setbacks. Your ability to adapt and persevere might mean everything in a world of uncertainty and difficulties.

Resilience and Decision-making:

- Embracing Uncertainty: Because decisions frequently involve stumbling through unfamiliar seas, life is essentially uncertain. With resilience, you can face uncertainty head-on and do it without fear.
- Learning from Failure: Being resilient allows you to see failure not as a roadblock but rather as a stepping stone. Any choice becomes a chance for

improvement and education, regardless of how it turns out.

- Staying Composed: Emotions can run high when faced with challenging situations. Your ability to remain calm and avoid letting emotions impair your judgment is aided by resilience.

- Adapting to Change: You can adjust to shifting conditions if you're resilient. It is occasionally necessary to modify or completely revise judgments. To handle such changes, resilient people are more suited.

Cultivating Resilience:

- Self-awareness: Recognize your positive and negative attributes. Your self-awareness makes it easier for you to identify situations where resilience could be required.

- Mindset: Develop a growth mindset, which sees obstacles as chances to improve. Frame setbacks as lessons learned rather than failures.
- Social Support: When faced with challenging decisions, rely on your social network. A fresh viewpoint and emotional support might be obtained by discussing your worries with close friends or family members.
- Self-care: Give self-care activities like physical activity, mindfulness, and sufficient rest a high priority. Resilience is supported by mental and emotional health.

- Positive Self Talk: Develop the habit of talking positively to yourself. In times of uncertainty or struggle, encourage oneself.

The Resilient Decision-maker:

Although they are not immune to challenges, resilient decision-makers are better prepared to deal with them. Making brave decisions, getting over setbacks, and adjusting to life's ever-changing circumstances are all made possible through resilience. You may empower yourself to live your life with confidence and a sense of direction by cultivating this quality.

Navigating Life Transitions with Confidence

Every transition in life, from significant turning points to unforeseen shifts, is a transition. A key component of taking control of your life is navigating these adjustments with confidence.

Understanding Life Transitions:

- Types of Transitions: Career changes, relationship changes, relocation, health issues, and other experiences can all be considered life transitions. They could be anticipated or unplanned.

- Impact on Decision-making: Choosing whether to accept the change, adapt, or look for new chances is frequently necessary throughout transitions. The effectiveness of the change may depend on how you handle these decisions.

Strategies for Navigating Transitions:

- Self-reflection: Allow yourself some thought time when transitioning. The change should be compared to your values, aspirations, and life goals.

- Seek Support: Lean on your support system to seek assistance. You can get advice and emotional support through transitions from friends, family, mentors, and counselors.

- Establish Specific Objectives: For the transition, establish specific goals. What do you want to get out of this transformation or what do you want to learn? The presence of goals can inspire and give direction.

- Stay Adaptable: Unexpected surprises and difficulties frequently accompany transitions. Navigating these turns and turns requires resilience and agility.
- Plan Carefully: Make a well-considered plan for scheduled transitions. Think about potential difficulties and backup plans, and be prepared to modify your strategy as necessary.
- Be Open to Learning: Take the chance to grow during transitions. Even the most challenging transitions can provide important lessons about life.

Confidence in Uncertainty:

A combination of self-assurance and adaptability is what gives one the confidence to deal with life adjustments. It's normal to feel uneasy about change, but if you take a proactive and upbeat stance, you'll be more comfortable making shifts.

Taking Charge:

In the end, taking charge of your life entails deliberately interacting with transitions rather than passively reacting to them. You may successfully maneuver life's always changing environment by being aware of their effects on your journey, using practical tactics, and remaining resilient.

Conclusion

This book's pages have served as a canvas on which we have painted the complex tapestry of life while delving into the profound art of saying "yes" and "no," of establishing boundaries, and of making decisions that uphold our ideals and goals.

We have created a story of self-empowerment and self-discovery via our reflections, insights, and anecdotes. I've discussed the insights, knowledge, and experiences that have helped me define what it means to be in charge of one's life.

The real beauty of this voyage, however, is not only found in the words that appear here; it is also found in the change that has occurred within myself. Each chapter's writing revealed to me that I was developing and becoming more aware of the subtleties of my own existence. I once again realized the value of resiliency, the significance of self-awareness, and the enormous influence of our decisions.

The moral of the narrative is that we have the power to control our own destiny, regardless of where we begin. The path through life may be filled with obstacles and unknowns, but it also abounds in opportunity and moments of extraordinary beauty.

I therefore do so with a heart full of thanksgiving as I finish this chapter of our journey together. I appreciate you allowing me to participate in your journey of self-awareness and empowerment and for letting me be a part of it.

The ability to take control of your life is firmly in your hands once you exit these pages and reenter the world. Set limits that respect your wellbeing, embrace each "yes" and "no" with intention, handle changes with fortitude, and, most importantly, have faith in your ability to create a life that clearly aligns with your highest goals and values.

The voyage has just begun; this is not the conclusion of the journey. Go forth and continue to make great decisions that will help you tell your life's story in a purposeful and confident manner.

Made in the USA
Coppell, TX
23 January 2024